Thinking Outside The Box

How to Think Creatively By Applying Critical Thinking and Lateral Thinking

Bruce Walker

Contents

Thinking Outside The Box

Introduction

What is Thinking Outside The Box?

How the Phrase Even Came to Be? (9 Dots Puzzle)

How Creative Are You? Quiz

How to Use this Book

Chapter 1: The Invisible Trap of Social Standards

Comfort Zone or Stagnation?

Chapter 2: Kicking the Box Open and Sparking your Creativity

Best Way to Active Your Creative Thoughts

Chapter 3: Lateral Thinking is the Key

Taking One Idea at a Time

Chapter 4: Applying Critical Thinking to Understand your Life Value

The Internet and Critical Thinking

Analyzing Problems without Emotions Involved

Steps to Critical Thinking

Chapter 5: Activities that force you to think outside the box

How to Naturally Start to Think Outside The Box

Conclusion

Introduction

The Difference Between The Rich and The Poor

The Power of Imitation

What You'll Discover in this Book

Chapter 1: Habits of the Rich and the Poor

Bad Habits and the Downward Spiral

The Upward Spiral

Changing the Direction of the Spiral

Chapter 2: Turning thoughts into reality: It All Starts with the Subconscious Mind

What is the Subconscious Mind?

How Successful People Put the Subconscious to Work

How Did you get to this Point?

Exercises to Direct the Power of your Subconscious

Introduction

"Thinking outside the box".

It's a phrase that has been used for nearly forty years now. For many in the corporate world, it has become a cliché -- so much so, you've problem heard it in any number of commercials. That doesn't mean the idea behind it isn't a powerfully useful instrument for your daily life, because it is.

Despite its overuse as a term, it's without a doubt one of the most potent methods you can improve the quality of your life, gain more time -- and even begin dipping your feet into the waters of your dream career.

You may assume that since out of the box thinking is such a cliché in the business world that it has no place in your personal life. Think again. Cliché or not it's still one of the most valuable and necessary assets many of us have -- even if we don't know it's bubbling just below the surface of our consciousness.

Consider the term "life hacks" which has caught on with people on the internet in the past few years. It's nothing more -- or should we say nothing less - than thinking out of the box. Have a space problem in your home that needs to be solved or you'll be sleeping on the front porch because you're out of room in your bedroom? Nothing less than out of the box thinking may help you keep your stash of precious items and allow you to sleep in your bed tonight.

Out of the box thinking implies a marvelous twist of the mind. It levels the playing field between you and the likes of Albert Einstein, Steve Jobs, and Thomas A. Edison. We're not saying you're about to create the next great computer, the latest revolutionary theory of the universe or something that will replace the electric light bulb. But you'll be able to turn your personal life on its head and begin to love life again.

What is Thinking Outside The Box?

In a nutshell, the phrase means to tackle a problem with creative or novel thinking, attacking the situation from an unusual or unexpected perspective. Take, for example, the cliché we've all heard: When life hands you lemons, make lemonade. That's out of the box or creative thinking. Taken one level higher, the thinker who kicks the box to the side of the road is the one who after making lemonade, launches his own multimillion-dollar lemonade business.

Some of the nation's most successful industrialists and entrepreneurs have been thinking creatively -- viewing problems from a perspective other business people couldn't or wouldn't think of. Thomas Edison, who nearly single-handedly drove the Industrial Revolution in the early twentieth century once said: "It's hard to think about achieving the impossible when you're surrounded with people wanting to discuss only the possible."

He probably found more inventions and innovations on the road to creating something else than most inventors or industrialists. One idea inevitable led to another. He, in effect, refused to limit his thinking to the conventional way of doing

Then there's Albert Einstein. Most people don't consider scientists as being very creative. But if anyone could prove that stereotype wrong, it would be Einstein. Asked how he came up with the theory of relativity. He first imagined himself riding a beam of light, traveling at 186,000 miles per second. Have you ever thought of that?

You're sitting back in your chair right now, thinking, "But I'm no Thomas Edison and definitely no Einstein." That very well could be true, but have you ever really put yourself to the test? Have you ever tried to put creative thought into your daily life?

But for your purposes -- especially if you're not used to putting such creativity into your thinking -- your thought process doesn't need to be such a dramatic change of perspective. Something as simple as repurposing an unused ladder into a unique-looking bookcase is a perfect example of thinking out of the box.

You can use this creative approach to any aspect of your life. Yes, you can. Don't think it takes any special education. Don't believe that you have to label yourself "creative" in any way to be able to think creatively.

Many individuals mistakenly believe that only writers, actors, and artists are creative. What they fail to take into account that all of us, in our ways, can be creative -- whether we recognize it at the moment or not.

There must be something that you'd like to view from a different perspective in your life -- from changing your economic position to learning a new set of life skills, to being more content with your surroundings. After all, if you're curious about the idea of "thinking outside of the box," then you're probably eager to give it a try.

How the Phrase Even Came to Be? (9 Dots Puzzle)

The origins of the phrase are fuzzy, but one thing is known. It comes from what's referred to as the "nine-dot" puzzle. Arrange nine dots on a piece of paper so there are three rows of three dots each. Now you can visualize what this puzzle looks like. Individuals were asked to connect the dots without lifting their pencil from the paper *and* ensuring that all nine dots are used.

Most individuals who try this, think that the lines they're drawing must stay within the confines the "box" the outer dots have created. But if you read the instructions again, that's not specified anywhere. Once you begin to think out of the confines of the box the dots created then you can find multiple solutions to the puzzle.

Go ahead and draw those nine dots right now and give it a try. What's impossible when you think one way suddenly becomes easy when you view it from a different perspective.

Are you an "out of the box" or a creative thinker? Below is a quick quiz to test your ability to do just that. You'll find the questions first. Following the questions, are the answers with a rough generalization of where your thinking aligns. The answers as well as a rough evaluation of your current level of creative thought are revealed below the quiz. (Don't get nervous! Approach this quiz as a game!)

How Creative Are You? Quiz

1. I have five apples and I take away three. How many apples do I have?

2. A plane crashes on the border of Germany and Poland. Where do you bury the survivors?

3. A bus explodes on the US-Canada border. Where do you bury the dead?

4. In what sport are the shoes made of metal?

> Soccer
>
> Horseracing
>
> Badminton
>
> Basketball

5. John's mother has four children. Three of them are named April, May, and June. What's the name of her fourth child?

6. Is it legal for a man to marry his widow's sister?

7. A man built a rectangular house with a southern view on all four sides. He looked out the window and saw a bear. What color was the bear?

8. If you were alone on a deserted house at night and there were an oil lamp, a candle, and firewood and you only have one match, which would you light first?

9. A farmer has 15 cows. All but 8 die. How many cows does he have left?

10. You drove a bus leaving Canterbury with 35 passengers, dropped off 6 and picked up 2 at Eversham picked up 9 more at Sittingbourne, dropped off 3 at Chatham, and then drove on to arrive in London 40 minutes later, what color are the driver's eyes?

Answers:

1 3 apples

2. You don't bury survivors

3. In a cemetery

4. Horseracing

5. John

6. By definition, if the man has a widow, then the man is deceased.

7. The bear was white. It was a polar bear and the house was built at the North Pole.

8. The match

9. 8 cows

10 You're the driver.

Evaluate your Score

8 - 10 right. Congratulations! You're already a creative thinking. You can use this book to help boost your current seemingly natural ability.

6 - 7 You're not bad at thinking out of the box. Once you start reading this book, you'll be able to develop this skill even further.

5 and below. You haven't been called upon to use your creative thinking. This book will help you do a better job of thinking outside the box.

How to Use this Book

This book is easy enough to use. Read through the entire book once, if you can, before you start putting any of the exercises or ideas into action. Of course, if you can't wait to put your new-found creativity into action, by all means, feel free to do so while the urge and desire are ignited.

What will you discover in this book to help you polish your innovation? You'll learn the essential exercises to spark your creative approach to problem-solving and how you can use this to your advantage. You'll be surprised at how many of the successful business people already know -- but seldom talk about -- thinking outside of the box.

Along those same lines, you'll discover exactly what lateral thinking is and how using this can help you find more creative solutions to your everyday problems -- the big ones and the smaller irritations.

You'll also learn that as much as creative or out of the box thinking is required on a daily basis, you can't put it into effect efficiently without using lateral and critical thinking processes alike. That's why there are chapters devoted to reminding you exactly what these are.

Are you ready to start a new life -- one of being free of "the boxed thinking" that may be holding you back? Then you need to start reading Chapter 1 right now.

Chapter 1: The Invisible Trap of Social Standards

Mary sat with her friends at the cafe. They were talking about their daily routines. "Sometimes I just get tired, believe it or not, of doing the same thing day after day. Don't get me wrong. I love my family and I wouldn't change them for the world. But, sometimes, I just think I need some spice in my life." She paused a moment and added. And I don't mean an affair."

Is that how you feel about your life? Do you look back at your high school days and even college days and think back to how much more creatively you thought back then? If you wanted to pack your suitcase and head for a trip to New York City or San Francisco or just wander aimlessly for a weekend, you'd do it.

Today, if you tried that there would probably a chorus of a thousand voices telling you socially responsible people just don't do that. You have to plan these things out. You have to make sure you get the right airline ticket price. And God forbid you to take your car. What would happen if it broke down?

Even if you haven't yearned to travel you're probably like most of us, you approach it from just about every aspect of your life from "the box." Most of us are rather satisfied with this life. Many individuals refer to this as their comfort zone. It's the area or activity in which they feel at ease.

This is the zone in which we accept who we are in life and where we are. After all, wasn't this the purpose of growing up and becoming an adult, to fit into society with a minimum of disturbance? And having a "comfort zone" is much better than constantly feeling anxious, feeling as if something bad is about to happen, but not knowing when or even why.

Comfort Zone or Stagnation?

But there's also a danger in that comfort zone and it's called *stagnation.* With that content, for some, comes the inability to see life any differently than what it is right now.

There's a theory that you're the average of the five people you associate with. What that usually means is you've adopted the social standards of these people. You've either adopted their interests or sought these friends and kept them because of your shared interests, similar careers or any other number of reasons. Support groups, by the way, are built on this concept.

If your friends are video gamers, for example, you're far more likely to be one as well. If they're interested in crafting, the chances are good that you'll be interested in that hobby too.

And that is where the "box" comes in. As long as you're following the social standards of the group spend time with, you're probably not thinking outside of the box -- you may not even recognize that you're in a box. You certainly don't consider yourself "trapped." Or perhaps you do.

Either way, you're reading this book, which is probably an indication you're interested in jumping out of your box and getting out of your comfort zone. Why is it difficult for many of us to step out of our comfort zone, think outside of the box and think differently from the rest of the group?

When was the last time you stopped to think about what you really wanted -- and still want -- out of the life? Do you allow yourself to dream about an awesome vacation or start writing that blog? Do others shoot your thoughts down right away, telling you it's a waste of time? So you return to your comfort zone and working within your box.

You do know it doesn't have to be that way, don't you? You can defy social standards and begin to do the things you've always wanted to do, the way you wanted to do them.

So, what's stopping you -- besides those so-called friends? Sure, their intentions are sincere, but ultimately you have to do what you feel is best for you. If you're weary of playing video games with them, tired of facing another scrapbook party without moaning and groaning about it or even can't take another episode of some "true crime" television show, then it's time to examine what's holding you back.

Here are several reasons why most of us are fearful of looking at life from any perspective than the one we've always have, that is our box.

1. **But we've always done it this way.**

Have you ever seen this sentiment in a poster: "But, we've always done it this way." That is the biggest reason people resist change. In effect, they're saying that everything is perfectly fine the way it is. You'll hear this same sentiment expressed as "Why change horses in midstream?" This is their way of rationalizing their efforts to stay within their comfort zone.

You may have even heard the saying "If it ain't broke, why fix it?" These people are conveying the exact sentiment. The general opinion is that if something -- anything -- has served us well for so long, "don't rock the boat.". When you do try to change things or "fix" things, you may be making things even worse.

2. Trapped by your own personal method of thinking.

You along with everyone else around you may be locked into a familiar, comfortable way of thinking. Up until this moment, you may never have even thought about doing anything differently. Why is everyone around you is doing basically the same things and they seemed perfectly satisfied? Your dissatisfaction, you presume, only means there's something wrong with you -- not with the social norms.

Because of this, you approach your problems from a limited point of view. Of course, we have always done it this way -- who am I to even dream of doing it another way. You can blame your "inner critic" for censoring your potential "out of box thinking."

3. Trapped by your emotions.

Stepping into the realm of creativity -- especially if you haven't been thinking in that way for a while -- can be intimidating, to say the least. As you've already seen, you find yourself straying from your comfort zone. That leads you into an uncomfortable realm. It's here you're more than likely begin to feel a general anxiety growing. As you begin to think differently, you're entering an unknown world, filled with "what if" incidents. What if, one of those options you're considering is less than optimal?

Or worse yet, what if you take this momentous step and your friends and family think you weird? What, if after all is said and done, the outcome is embarrassing to you -- or even painful in some way?

What you may not realize that all of these emotions are just different ways your body resists change. It's hoping that you'll eventually cave into these fears and qualms and just plain procrastinate on this concept -- whatever it may be.

4. It's hard to be creative with personal problems hanging over your head.

If you're beating yourself up because you can't, for the life of you, think outside of the box, you may want to stop and examine your life for a moment. Are you going through some personal crisis or problem? It's hard to be creative when you're struggling with a major life change. You may be experiencing financial hardships at the moment or even going through an emotional event like a divorce. At these or similar points in your life, it's all most of us can do to just hold our own with the life we have.

Sometimes, though, this is the time when you may be digging up some of the oldest and deepest held regrets about what you *didn't* do with your life and you begin to daydream about "what might have been."

If this is the case, you still may want to wait to make any type of creative changes in your life. If you ignore these issues and continue to plow through with trying to be creative anyway, you may be just setting yourself up for failure.

5. Searching for the "right" answer

You've probably learned this habit in school. Every question, according to the tests you've taken in school, has either a right or wrong answer. Think about the how many true and false tests you've taken and how many multiple choice quizzes you've sat through. After approaching an education in this fashion, you may discover your creativity stilted, at least initially, by considering whether what you're planning falls in one of these two categories either right or wrong.

Without a doubt, there are advantages to this categorization habit, but it does nothing to further your creative thinking. Right about now, you may be thinking that a three-week vacation to New York City is in order. But one of your dearest friends tells you this isn't the right time. That's not the proper decision right now.

Never mind the fact that this might be the "right" answer for you to clear your mind for a while. Or perhaps you've made a decision on some other aspect of your life, but here again, someone or your instincts tell that isn't the "right" answer for you.

It hinders your "out of the box" thinking. Once you realize that the vast majority of issues we deal with on a daily basis can't be viewed in either black or white. There is a spectrum of shades of gray that can lead you to happiness. Issues that pop up in real life usually have more than one answer. When someone tries to assign a right or wrong way to a problem or try to impose one on you, they're missing the valued concept that the issue may have more than one "right" answer.

6. Viewing creative, outside of the box thinking as "destructive."

Here me out on this one. Perhaps you don't even realize you're thinking this, it may be so ingrained and enmeshed in your thinking. If you choose a different way of doing even something as simple as changing your morning routine, your subconscious may feel that it's being a destructive force in the world. After all, if someone wanted to point at you and accuse you of ripping the fabric of society as we know it apart, he might be right. "Rules," they may say "are that simple and are created for a reason. Who are you to deviate from them? What makes you special?"

You may believe, at first glance, that this is a block that makes little or no sense. But you'd be amazed at how many individuals follow all the rules, even though they aren't working for them. There's a person I spoke to once who said before she takes any specific actions she asks herself, "How does this serve me?" If it doesn't serve her -- make her life better in some way -- she tosses that "rule" aside. Step by step, she's remaking her life in a very creative way, by thinking out of your own box.

Have you noticed that that people praise and admire some of the most creative thinkers in the business world? Think about Richard Branson and his marvelous success and the brave moves he made to make it happen. But they refuse to break even a small rule in their life. Perhaps you should think twice before you start admiring someone like Branson -- and start breaking some rules of your own.

Seriously. Are you ready to consider not only thinking outside of the box, but actually kicking it wide open and allowing some truly creative thoughts into your life? Then you're ready to move to the next chapter. That's where we'll get the process moving.

.

Chapter 2: Kicking the Box Open and Sparking your Creativity

Many people get excited about the idea of thinking outside of the box and kick it to the curb immediately only to discover that after years of conventional thinking, it's a bit more difficult than they had imagined. And that makes sense. After years of thinking one way, it's not easy to allow your mind to be "liberated" and allow it to run wild.

Before you attempt to jump into creative thinking, you may want to "exercise your brain." Don't worry, these aren't as tough as you may believe. It's hard to start thinking in a manner you're not accustomed to.

To be truthful, that's not your fault. So don't beat yourself up if the creative thoughts don't flow immediately. Your brain has been used to thinking in a certain manner and it will take some time for it to rewire itself and adjust to another thought process. It'll be slow going at first, but as you continue to do it, your brain catches on and works faster at it. Guaranteed.

Your brain is no different from any other muscle in your body. If you don't use, then it slowly gets weaker. That's the bad news. The good news, though, is that it's easy enough to strengthen this muscle just as you would any other one in your body: through regular exercise.

At first, when your "creative thinking muscles" are initially called into action after perhaps years of unused, you may turn around and find yourself wandering aimlessly through your house, wondering where and how to begin this valuable thought process.

Many fiction writers find that every morning upon arising they need to get their "creative juices" flowing by writing three to five pages of . . . well, nothing. Their goal is to write anything that pops into their minds. Hopefully, some of this covers what their subconscious minds have unearthed while they slept. But if they can't recall what they dreamed of or any words that came mind then basically, they're instructed to write anything. It may be something as simple as "I need my morning coffee."

Once they clear their minds and got their neurons moving at full speed, they inched themselves out of their box and into their projects, whatever those may be. Believe it or not, it works more often than not.

Best Way to Active Your Creative Thoughts

If you're not by nature a writer, you obviously you won't need to do this (although it still may be a wonderful creative exercise for you as well). But if you're not interested in writing, here are few alternatives that may help channel your creativity more efficiently.

Alphabetize your Words

Okay, they don't have to be *your* words but once you discover this exercise, you may very well become addicted to it. It forces you to look at words in a different light, which can only help you begin to look at not only words differently, but the entire world around you from a new perspective.

Begin by picking a word, any word will do. It may be one you've just noticed on a billboard while you're driving or something you discover on a magazine cover. Now instead of looking at it with your physical eyes, look at it with your mind. What you're about to do is rearrange the letters so that they're placed in your mind in alphabetical order and not as the word is spelled.

If the word is "number," then you'd rearrange the letters like this: b-e-m-n-r-u. This makes your mind use all the information, but just rearrange them. Don't just settle for doing it once a day, though. Remind yourself to do it throughout the day. Consider doing this up to five times a day.

When you first start off, you may want to choose short words. This activity is a bit harder than you may think. As you conquer words that are three to five letters long, then you'll graduate to ever longer words. There's no need to push yourself, you'll discover that if you just allow this to happen, you'll have more fun. And part of thinking creatively certainly involves fun.

Another note for you to think about. No one needs to know what you're doing if you don't want to tell them.

Adding a series of one-digit numbers as quickly as you can

This is another exercise that on the surface doesn't seem to have any connection to creative thinking or thinking outside of the box, but after you do this for a while, you'll discover how your synapses move more quickly. That's a sure sign, you'll be thinking creatively without even having to think about it.

Take a series of one-digit numbers, from zero to nine. Place these numbers in any order you care to. Now, without using a calculator, start adding up the numbers -- as quickly as you can. The beauty of this exercise is that it forces you to constantly change the information you're juggling in your mind. As you're adding this total, your mind needs to focus solely on the current grand total -- and then as you become faster at this -- another grand total quickly. Talk about making your brain agile.

Basically what you're doing is inputting some essential information into your mind and then deleting it -- replacing it with another "grand total" as you add more numbers -- and so it continues. The perfect time to do this? When you're standing in the grocery line. You can easily add up the numbers to one of the dollars of five dollar bills you have in your pocket or just as easily take the numbers from your purchases and use those numbers -- in no particular order.

Before you realize it you're performing this action faster and faster. But the true goal of this exercise is to limber up your creative thinking.

Running for creativity.

Now, this suggestion may be the most confusing of all. It is for many individuals. On the surface, it really is difficult to see how the creative process is connected to exercising. But running is wonderful because it stimulates your whole body, producing the chemical called *serotonin*. It's been called the "chemical form" of happiness. Its long been known by scientists and medical doctors to be responsible for that "runner's high" so many individuals talk about.

Once you hit that "runner's high" your mind is capable of seeing things from a different perspective. You're much more likely to see the whole picture of the issue. Researchers now agree that the combination of what many call "the runner's point of view" and the increased blood flow pumping throughout your body actually improves your concentration. This is especially helpful, because your mind is churning out solutions and ideas that only you can perceive.

Carry a notebook

This may be simple, but power habits you can develop to encourage yourself to think outside the box. Carry a notebook. All the time. No exceptions. Have you ever come up with an idea and say to yourself, "Awesome. I'm sure I'll remember this." By the time you get home or to someplace to write this idea down, it's slipped your mind, with no guarantee to return.

It may be that none of the ideas one day are extremely useful. But that "not-so-useful" idea may lead you to another wonderfully useful thought that may be the one to change your life.

Eat dark chocolate and walnuts

You have to wonder how this suggestion can possibly affect your ability to think outside of the box. But, even if it doesn't, it's a tremendous method of rewarding yourself. If you don't like walnuts, don't worry about it. You can eat Brazil nuts or almonds and get the same creative effect.

Why would dark chocolate and nuts increase your creativity? You can thank the rich and abundant supply of antioxidants found in this combination of sweets. These wonderful substances enable your blood to flow to the brain more swiftly which in turn improves your concentration.

Additionally, the nuts are a great source of vitamin E which prevents poor memory and increases your concentration levels. By the way, eating this combination of food also increases your happiness.

Adopt the Beginner's Mind

You may believe you're ready to tackle the world with your out of the box thinking. But there's still one more exercise you'll want to think about while you're using these activities. It's called adopting the beginner's mind. At least that's what the Buddhists call it.

Some people refer to as a looking at life through the eyes of a child. You can call it whatever you desire. The idea is to empty your mind of everything you believe you know about your world and how everything around you operates and look at your surroundings as if you've never seen any of it before.

Remember when you were a child, anything and everything was possible? Think back, too, to when your children were younger, they too saw the world with eyes of wonder. Absolutely nothing is impossible. And that's exactly how you should be looking at your world in order to think outside of the box.

Don't feel constrained by what worked in the past or what gave you grief. Try it again. It just may work this time. And even if it doesn't, it may be the idea that leads you to the one that will actually change your life.

This is more difficult than you may believe and it may be one of those exercises you need to repeat not only daily but several times a week. Eventually, you'll come to every issue with a "beginner's mind," realizing you really don't know anything about the issue. Finding a creative answer is so much easier this way.

Here is an exercise in what it feels like to look at things around you with a beginner's mind. Gather the following items: a coffee mug, pen, and paper. Yes, that's all you'll need. To have a really good time doing this, you may want to invite a few friends to join you.

Place the cup on the table. Give yourself -- and your friends -- a specific amount of time. It's best to set a timer, then no one has to stop to watch the clock as the minutes tick by. You know that a coffee cup's purpose is to drink out of.

But what else could it be used for? You've seen people use them as pen and pencil holders among other things. List as many of these uses as possible. The goal is not to limit your thinking. If your first thought is a house for a mouse, write it down. The sky's the limit.

Walk Away from the Problem

Seems counter-intuitive now doesn't it? But it works, nearly every time. Walking away -- either literally or figuratively -- and clearing your mind for a few minutes seems to clear the mind enough to allow your subconscious mind crank some idea out.

Try it and you'll see. This trick works probably for the same reason that you get your best ideas in the shower. You're allowing your mind to clear and busy with an activity that is done by rote memory.

Anything that makes your mind relax and "digest" the problem, as it were, helps you to think creatively.

You're almost ready to apply creative thinking in your daily life. There are only a few more steps you should know about before you can expect great success from your "out-of-the-box" thought processes.

In the next chapter, you'll discover how a thought process called "lateral thinking" can work hand in hand with creative thinking to help you take that grand leap out of the box.

Chapter 3: Lateral Thinking is the Key

Consider this list of statements. Don't judge them initially, just read them.

Before the earth was round, it was flat.

Before the earth revolved around the sun, the universe revolved around the earth.

Before we all became aware of Einstein's laws of gravity and his other theories, we were only aware that the universe was operating from Newtonian physics.

What changed? Did some god from heaven decide to change the rules on us? No, our perception -- our knowledge changed. And that changed the way we viewed everything. But more importantly, by changing the way we thought about the universe, it opened up an entirely new view of the universe.

In other words, someone, somewhere starting applying lateral thinking and in the process literally introduced the rest of us to a new universe.

Let's take a quick look at the shape of the earth. Flat as a pancake. That's what the ancient cavemen thought. For thousands of years, that was the standard norm. How could it be anything else? All you had to do was look around you. Except for hills and mountains, everything around you was flat.

Certainly, you can see why it was so easy to believe the earth was flat. It was the only common sense answer. If the earth were round, then that means someone on the opposite side of the earth of you were standing "upside down." (Because you certainly weren't!)

Then, consciously or not, Pythagoras, applied lateral thinking to this fact. He took this fact and his ideas slowly branched off of the facts as the world knew them.

The same laterally thinking was applied to the earth being the center of the universe to the earth revolving around one of a myriad of suns in the universe. Again, that's lateral thinking in action.

What? You say you aren't a Galileo, a Newton or an Einstein? Who among us is? But that doesn't mean you can't apply lateral thinking in your own life.

Before you jump total out of the box and think as if no box existed, you may want to test the waters, so to speak, simply by peering over the edge of the top of the box. In many ways, it can be considered an intermediate step between following the status quo and society's standards in your decisions and jumping outside of the box.

Taking One Idea at a Time

It's true that lateral thinking is a method of solving problems -- whether they involve a new way of folding your bed sheets or establishing world peace. What distinguishes itself from the other two form of thought process is that it not only allows for creativity, but also uses reasoning that isn't always that obvious and may not be available if you use the traditional step-by-step logic.

First coined in 1967 by Edward de Bono, lateral thinking is neither the traditional vertical logic we learned in high school and college no the "horizontal" imagination you probably associate with individuals in the more creative imagination. The latter is usually characterized by the individuals being endowed with a myriad of ideas, but not really caring about the feasibility of their implementation.

Lateral thinking also differentiates itself from what's known as critical thinking, which is mainly used in the judgment of the true value of statement or seeking errors in the thought process. By contrast, the more you learn about lateral thinking, the more you'll discover is about learning and revealing the "movement value" of statements and concepts.

You'll learn to discover those individuals who are employing lateral thinking because they're capable of moving from one known idea to branching off new concepts from the known and creating new ideas. Every idea, in this form of thought processing, is creating a branch of the original one.

According to de Bono, the human mind uses four types of thinking tools:

1. **Idea-generating tools.**

These are the tools that actually break into your current thinking patterns, regardless of how long you've been "stuck" in this mental rut. It's the way you generate tools in order to jump-start yourself out of outdated routine patterns and other ideas you may be holding about the status quo.

2. Focus tools

These are valuable instruments intended to broaden your search parameters. The focus tools, as de Bono sees them, aid you in *where* to search for new ideas. Sometimes ideas just come to us out of the blue sky, but more often than not, we need to put some effort into searching for them. As you focus on one action or one invention, your mind suddenly, even abruptly, moves laterally and you realize that something that works for one innovation, can easily be transferred to another project.

3. Harvest tools

These tools are properly named. These instruments of lateral thinking ensure that the ideas you've gathered are "harvested," kept so that they can be used later. As you can imagine, harvesting, as it's called many times, is used at the end of the thought process of thinking session.

Its goal is to "bank" any and all ideas that may prove valuable to apply to the problem later. It's easy to overlook or skip this segment, thinking it's not that necessary. But by ensuring that you harvest the ideas generated you're free to use them at any time you deem necessary.

Harvesting also helps you to identify specific ideas that could be used immediately as well as those that have potential but may need some polishing and refining before you put them to use.

This process also generates some "common sense" thinking into the process. Very often, an individual or group generates excitement around an idea and implements it before its time. By using the harvesting approach, you can stash these ideas away instead of rushing into major commitments. It forces you to look at the long-term so you can make the most of your "yield" of new thoughts.

4. Treatment tools

According to de Bono, treatment tools, in the long run, promote and support the consideration of constraints found in the real world. These type of tools also take into consideration the resources with which you have to work as well as the support you may have. One of the most valuable of these tools is an exercise called "shaping."

In this one, you take the raw idea and shape it to the specifications you need in your project or to solve your problem.

Examples of Lateral Thinking: From Edward de Bono Himself

Edward de Bono himself admits that many of the definitions and descriptions of lateral thinking on the internet today are nothing at all what he intended it to be. For some individuals trying to envision lateral thinking these sometimes conflicting descriptions may cause you confusion -- and rightly so.

But de Bono provides you with several eye-opening examples of lateral thinking and what it's not through a series of simple phrases:

1. **You can't dig a hole in a different spot by digging the same hole deeper and deeper.**

Think about it. What de Bono means by this is that you're not going to find the answer to your problem by just pushing harder in the same direction. Some industrialists have said the same thing by saying that the same type of thinking which caused the problem in the first place isn't going to solve it. It may be time to start digging somewhere else or thinking in other directions.

If you're serious about solving the problem or creating a different outcome than what's staring at your right now, you'll need to pick up the shovel again and start digging in another spot.

You've no doubt heard of the story of the man who is under the streetlamp in the middle of the night searching for the $100 bill he lost. A police officer found him and asks what he is doing and the man tells the officer, the police officer generously offers to help.

After a short time, the officer asks the gentleman if he's sure he lost the money here. The man, with a matter of fact shrug of his shoulders, replies, "Heck, no! I lost the bill over there." He points to a darkened spot on the sidewalk." Then as if anticipating the police officer's next question, continues, "But it's too dark to see anything over there, so I thought I would look here." It's the same idea. The gentleman refuses to "dig his hole" in a more profitable location. Instead, he keeps digging under the light, thinking what he's searching for will miraculously show up.

2. You use lateral thinking when you need to change ideas and perceptions.

When you start thinking logically, you obviously begin with a specific set of circumstances and ingredients laid out in front of you. Think of a chess board with all the pieces in their proper places. If you know how to play and you're pinned against another good player, you'll immediately know that all the moves are logical. In fact, you can take your turn and be reasonably sure of what your opponent will do after that.

Many of the best chess players, then, thinking many moves in advance, based on the logic of the game can outwit their opponent and ultimately win the game.

The problem with this type of thinking, de Bono contends is that the "chess pieces" we assume we have may not even exist. Imagine for a moment, a young toddler who comes upon a chess board and replaces the chess pieces, with his own toys. Now, the rules of the game have changed and the same logic of the traditional chess game don't apply.

And in a very real sense, that's what lateral thinking is all about. It's not about playing the game with the same pieces. Rather it's about changing the pieces and challenging your mind to look at the game differently.

In other words, its emphasis is on the perception of the game, not the actual implementation. The real beauty of lateral thinking is that it allows you to organize the world around you into pieces that work for you -- or pieces you need -- to be able to process them in a fashion which makes sense.

It might be obvious, but consider this for a moment. Breakthroughs in new ways of thinking are only possible when you toss the old assumptions aside. Once you get rid of "it's the way we always thought," then you can more clearly see how the pieces may fall into place differently. Like the chessboard with all the traditional pieces will produce the same response with us, you'll respond differently if you place the green plastic "army men" of your youth on the squares. It's the time to make new rules.

For example, consider the work of Pablo Picasso. Without a doubt, he broke all the rules of art when he began experimenting with his personal style. To some, his actions were sacrilegious. To others, they were brilliant and allowed other artists to think in entirely new dimensions.

If you're like most people, though, this is difficult to do. Your "default thinking" as some individuals call it is still "linear thinking." Don't despair, though, because the "we've-always-done-it-this-way-thinking" can be overridden.

Below are several marvelous examples of how to stamp out linear thinking right in front of your eyes and begin to see the world in more "lateral" arrangement.

Start off by listing all the assumptions in the problem.

Yes, this may seem simplistic, but it gets right to the heart of the problem. I knew a gentleman once who approached every electrical item that didn't work with the same first step: Make sure that it really is getting the electric source it needs to work.

From a computer to a lamp, to his car, he started with ensuring that whatever was powering that item was working. This was the first on his list of assumptions.

Whenever you're presented with what seems like an unfixable problem, list everything you already know about the situation -- then take off from there. Make sure that none of these assumptions are wrong, then you can extend your thinking from there.

Verbalize the problem

Basically, this means ask yourself, how every other person would approach the problem. In this way, you're detailing in very specific steps the most obvious solutions to solving the problem.

Look these over and then ask yourself this critical question, "What if I couldn't do this? Then what would happen?"

Now you're beginning to make yourself open to lateral thinking. If you can't solve the problems or get to the core of the idea through normal means, then you'll have to come up with a different perspective. When you first begin this exercise, you may find yourself shrugging your shoulders somewhat puzzled. But after a bit, this approach will become second nature. You'll truly see, at this point, that what others believed was a "problem" has now been transformed into an "opportunity" to see things from a different angle.

Question the original question

Sounds like a conundrum, doesn't it? Perhaps you're not finding the right answer because, ultimately, you're not asking the proper question. According to de Bono, your next question should be, "What if I could re-write the question?"

This helps your brain think differently and begin to see things from a different perspective. You'd be surprised how this works even with a simple search on the internet. If you continue to ask the same question into your search engine, you'll continue to get the same sites to review over and over again.

The moment you ask the question from a different perspective or using a few different words, new, sometimes more relevant sites pop up. The next thing you know, you're discovering more ideas. That's exactly what happens when you dare to question the question you're asking about the situation.

Start solving the problem from the end.

What? As crazy as that may sound, that's exactly what you need to do at the time in order to implement lateral thinking. More often than you can imagine, a problem is solved by working from the desired solution first.

Engineers often do this when they're making a new invention. They call it "reverse engineering."

What occurs the very moment you do this, you've stripped away all the details (at least the most cumbersome of them) which made you balk at the answer in the first place. Once you start at the end, your tendency to "overthink" the answer melts away.

Change your perspective of the problem.

Have you ever noticed when another person steps in to help solve the problems, somebody suddenly sees the pieces a bit differently? Why do you suppose this is? They are not already filled with the preconceived notions that you have from studying the problem so closely.

Think about how you use lateral thinking every day in your home life. There's a movement out there that encourages you to start using "hacks." A hack is nothing more than looking at an everyday object and repurposing it. Think about the many ladders you've seen on Pinterest that are now bookshelves. Or fifty-five gallon tubs that are used as containers in container gardening. These are simple examples of lateral thinking.

Recently, someone stripped away the contents of a used book (not a valuable first-edition one-of-a-kind book) and hid their internet router inside it. This was a hack to a problem. It was lateral thinking.

Many individuals, unfortunately put blinders on when they're trying to their problems -- or even create something new. They believe, for whatever reason that they only have two options. The first is to put your head down and plow on, pushing forward despite the obstacles. Depending on the problem and the situation, the only result you'll get is a headache.

The other choice is to spend as little effort on the problems as possible. This isn't an acceptable choice either. Cutting corners never created any lasting breakthroughs or sparked any revolutions. It barely gets you through the day.

So how do you solve your problems? Try hard work combined with just the right amount of mental flexibility. You have to put in the effort. But you also have to be open and nonjudgmental enough to know when it's time to try something else.

Chapter 4: Applying Critical Thinking to Understand your Life Value

Creativity. Out of the box thinking. Lateral thinking.

You may be wondering if there are any more methods left to approach a problem. As a matter of fact, there is one more way. That's by applying the concept of critical thinking to your set of problem-solving tools.

No doubt you've heard of it. You may also be tired of hearing of it. For most people, they have heard the phrase since they first entered high school and then moved on to college. It could be, though, that somewhere along the line of it being used repeatedly in your academic life or in your business careers, you've turned a deaf ear to what it really means.

It could be a quick review of the phrase and how you can apply it to your daily values may be in order. Briefly, it's the ability to think rationally and clearly so that you can fully comprehend and grasp the logical connection between ideas and concept.

You may think that you should be the norm for your thinking -- or anyone's way of thinking. You'd be surprised to learn that if you left the mind to wander aimlessly, how "uncritical" your thinking may end up.

You'd probably find -- as many scientists have -- that if you don't apply critical thinking to your thought patterns, many of your thoughts would end up biased, uninformed and sometimes just plain prejudiced -- not to mention distorted beyond belief.

You can hear this every day when a group of people gather for their morning coffee or breakfast. It's in these sessions that the individuals feel free enough to talk openly about their feelings from the state of the world to their spouse's refusal to see things their own way.

While some individuals use critical speaking when they talk, many simply just spill out their thoughts which have been formed quickly -- and you wonder if they are indelibly shaped forever -- by their emotions. They hear certain "facts" and simply don't take the time to check them out.

Instead of speaking from the position of knowledge, they very often speak from their gut. This isn't always an accurate reflection of the problem and even more often than not a less accurate reflection of any solid solutions.

You can probably see immediately the problem with this. The very quality of our lives and the results of what you do -- and everyone else does -- with their lives depend quite heavily on the quality of your thoughts. Inaccurate or non-critical thinking is not only costly in so many ways, but it can also cause permanent damage to your life. Long-term, non-critical thinking involving inaccurate ideas that make it almost impossible to tear down. Before you know it, you're living your life based on inaccurate accounts of the world.

That not only means the physical manifestations you bring about with this thinking may not only be skewed, but may also not be what you want to see in the world. Beyond that, you're putting your happiness, prosperity, and everything that goes along with it on the line. If you want to be able to produce something -- anything -- that is positive as a result of your life, you need to be able to think critically about it.

Looking at your weight, for example, and doing nothing but viewing it from a non-critical thought process will do little or nothing if you're trying to lose several pounds. You may end up talking yourself into the fact that it's impossible to do anything. Or you could have yourself talked into the fact that you are the only person to blame for that. You may also uncritically follow those thoughts to how "bad" of a person you are because you can't remedy the problem. As a result, you unwittingly contribute to your problem.

In a nutshell, in order for you to think critically about anything in your life, you must be capable of logical reasoning. Critical thinking, therefore, is all about being an active learner instead of a passive, unquestioning recipient of random bits of information you may have heard.

The Internet and Critical Thinking

Your daily interaction with the internet makes critical thinking all that much more vital in your life. Many people tend to start researching the net only to find inaccurate and downright false facts, but fail to question them -- even though their minds nag them that something isn't quite right.

That leads many people to pass on these inaccuracies and even hoaxes as serious stories. This, in turn, creates an avalanche of unthinking, unwitting acceptance. People accept these facts at face value and these falsehoods and hoaxes are now spoken as the truth. What's worse, they're repeated over and over as being the truth. The ability to treat all data with suspicion until you get the chance to reflect on them, research the information and think independently about them is the ultimate goal of every critical thinker.

Analyzing Problems without Emotions Involved

At this point, you're may be wondering about that. After all, it's not every day someone comes up to you on the street and asks that question. If you're at all unsure about whether you currently can think, reason and analyze the problems in your life, read about the characteristics a person who can do this possesses. If you can match your traits up to several of the abilities listed below, you're already performing some level of this form of thought on your own.

You're a critical thinker if you question the ideas and assumptions behind the beliefs.

Before accepting unconfirmed data and the word of others at face value, you need to question the basis of what they're saying and the source of their information. You, additionally, need to question the assumptions behind these statements as they're bandied about. Don't accept them at face value. Instead, see if the statements and the arguments which seem to bolster their credibility actually hold up under scrutiny.

As a critical thinker, you'll consistently search to ensure that the ideas presented to you and the underlying arguments for accepting them represent the entire picture. Ensure the validity before you accept them. Along with this, you'll want to keep your mind open and move on if, for some reason, they don't.

As a critical thinker, you'll not only be able to identify and analyze problems in a systematic way, you'll be able to solve them as well.

The alternative to this is to use your intuition or your gut feelings toward problem-solving. Certainly, there's nothing inherently wrong with this method. Some of the best decisions people ever made have been made from the use of the elusive intuition. Don't ever discard or diminish your intuition. It'll serve you well for the rest of your life. But, if your intuition isn't kicking in and you feel as if it's leaving you stranded or you just want to confirm it, then critical thinking can do this.

Understands the "link" between ideas, in other words, who can connect the dots, as they say.

Hmm. there are those dots again. Remember those nine dots you drew at the beginning of this book. You approached them no doubt from a critical perspective. And that was the first step. Critical thinking.

Far too many people -- from business executives to stay at home spouses -- can see all the dots, but they don't bother to find what they have in common. Think of the "dots" we've been talking about as facts. Instead of just accepting these facts as independent ideas and concept, begin to align them in such a way that you can form a cogent, logical argument out of them.

If you can do this properly, you'll be able to "connect the dots" so that you have an airtight solution to the dilemma.

Constantly Search for the Best Possible Conclusion

The bottom line is simple enough once you've stripped away everything else. This form of thinking -- very often highly valued in our society -- depends on how we view the variables involved in order to create the best solution possible given the circumstances at the moment.

In other words, you can be assured you're a critical thinker if your thought process is searching, scanning and possibly discarding ideas in order to develop the best possible conclusion at the moment.

This all sounds great, you say, but you're still not quite so sure about how to approach this critical thinking tool. Just as with anything else you use in your life -- from mathematics to reading and writing to riding a bicycle -- you'll have to use and hone the necessary skills. This sounds much harder than it really is.

You're about to discover that these skills cover a wide range, most of which you already possess and use in your daily life. They include, among other things, observation, interpretation, evaluation, explanation, problem solving and finally, decision making.

That may sound overwhelming at the moment, but it really isn't. Here is a short, but comprehensive description of how you can approach any concept or idea and apply critical thinking. It could be you've just never broken the process into separate steps -- yet.

Steps to Critical Thinking

If you following the steps outlined below, you'll be certain of applying all of your resources to viewing your circumstances, dilemma or problem with a critical eye.

1. Choose a topic then view it from an impartial point of view.
2. Discern what the various arguments are involved in this issue.
3. Develop a point of view to help you determine the validity and strength of the arguments
4. As you review this, consider what weaknesses or negative points you can identify in this particular way of thinking.
5. Determine what the implications are behind the statements or the argument being made.
6. Finally, provide a structured platform for reasoning and support for the argument you're planning on professing

Let's face it, none of us thinks along these lines every day, seven days a week. Sometimes the situation forces us to think in this way, sometimes we're not even sure why we're driven to question some arguments.

There are times, though, when emotions grip you and your ability to view events or situations through impartial eyes disappear into the thick of the night. We could be angry, suffering from grief or even overwhelmed with joy. Your ability to look at events rationally may dwindle. That's fine, as long as you know what's going on.

That's the bad news. The good news is that your capabilities to think on a critical level depend on your current mindset. If your mindset isn't laden with unnecessary emotions, you actually improve your ability to think rationally and critically.

Chapter 5: Activities that force you to think outside the box

These chapters have covered everything to get you started in kicking your creative thinking into high gear. At this moment you're leaps and bounds beyond what most people know about thinking outside of the box and probably light years ahead of most people about implementing that type of thinking into your daily life.

What? You don't feel as if you're ready yet to use this type of thinking efficiently and successfully. That's perfectly understandable. Remember that the more you use anything -- from the muscles of your body to knowledge -- the better you'll get at implementing it in your life.

Thinking outside the box is no different. But beyond that, there are tips, tricks, and techniques you can use to jumpstart your ability to thinks outside of the box. That's what this chapter is all about. It's written expressly to show you what you can do to boost this method of thought process.

Some of these ideas are easy to institute, others may require a bit more effort and may even involve some resources you might not have available to you at the moment. Then again, once you start thinking creatively you just might find yourself inventing a creative way to employ those that are "supposedly" beyond your reach.

How to Naturally Start to Think Outside The Box

The following list of activities are mere suggestions that have helped others view their circumstances differently in order to solve a problem or find a different, more efficient way to do an everyday action. Use those that are most valuable to you at the moment, but don't summarily discard the others. You'll never know when you'll be able to use them.

Travel

Expand your horizons. Isn't that what you were always told that travel would do for you? At the time you heard this, you may have wondered exactly what your "horizons" were, but you figured they probably did need to be expanded regardless.

It turns out, that the scientific study performed in this area, confirms this sentiment. Traveling -- especially abroad -- does indeed expand your horizons. And just for the record, improves your ability to think creatively. A recent study revealed that college students who traveled overseas scored higher on tests measuring creative thinking than those students who stayed on campus for the same time period.

Specifically, this study assessed American college students who traveled to England for a summer-study program. What causes this burst of creative thinking in students who went abroad? The obvious reason is the exposure they received to a variety of cultural norms. Regardless of your age, travelers are exposed to a society which performs activities and views problems differently from what's done in the states. That exposure alone sparks the idea that an act you may perform one way for so long could be done another way.

For some, the way one culture attacks its biggest problems of makes the most of the size of the space they have for certain events may trigger a creative chain reaction in your mind. The next thing you know, you're transferring that approach to your specific situations.

While the study didn't specifically state so, some experts in the field have extrapolated that the same conclusion probably holds true for traveling across the United States. With a country as large as this one, regional differences naturally exist. You may discover that something that you encounter in one city may help you with own personal problem-solving techniques.

So pack your bags and expand your horizons!

Talk to people you don't know

No one is telling you to put your life in danger and befriend a serial killer or a mass murderer. Talking to individuals you may pass by in your neighborhood coffee shop or restaurant or even laundromat can help boost your powers of creativity.

Again, just like above, you'll be seeing the world from another perspective -- theirs. Meeting these individuals, as you may well guess, is only the first step, though. The second and more critical step in this activity is to listen when they talk. That's the only way you'll be able to drink in their unique perspective on the world.

Viewing even mundane matters as political points from someone who has had different life experiences from yourself may help you understand how someone could hold that position. And that in itself may be the catalyst that sparks you to think outside of the box.

Break away from your daily routine

What? You've probably spent much effort and time disciplining yourself to create a routine to help boost your productivity. Now, you're being told to break from that routine that's worked so well for you.

Well, yes. You may want to break from it, but don't toss it out the window. If you're not focused on performing everything you have always done, in the same manner, you've always done it, then you may open yourself up to new options for doing things.

You may want to start with your morning commute. If you're like most of us, you tend to rely on the same route with the same traffic lights, making the same turns. You may even be seeing the same commuters driving the same cars on their way to work. And dare we say experiencing the same traffic jams day after day.

Why not start out a few minutes earlier and take a scenic route to work? The different type of landscape and just the need to pay attention to your route may help kindle your imagination. It may occur while you're driving. Suddenly you see something that can help solve a problem at work. Or you may have a spark of creativity later in the day because of this "creative detour."

Of course, there are numbers of ways to break from your routine either at work or at home. For women of an earlier generation, Monday was always "wash day," the day they gathered all the dirty clothes in the house and washed them. Similarly, Saturdays for that same generation of women was cleaning day. Floors would get scrubbed, bedrooms cleaned out and sweepers run throughout the entire house.

If Monday night is taco night at your house, why not surprise the entire family with a different menu? And who said that Thanksgiving Day and Christmas Day were all about turkey or ham? Why not call the best Chinese restaurant in town and eat Chinese on Christmas Eve? It'll not only be a Christmas to remember, it may just help you think outside of the box.

Constrain your thinking

You're presented with another suggestion that tends to be counter-intuitive. Normally, the average person thinks "creativity" and immediately associates it with freedom. Instead, go back to the adage that "necessity is the mother of invention."

What if you only had so many options? How could you piece them together in order to create something memorable, solve problems at home, or help build your business or career? If that sounds impossible, then it sounds as if you need to at least give it a try.

Counterintuitively, it turns out that constraints can actually increase our creative output. This could be due to removing the overwhelming of having too many choices. If you've ever faced the hurdle of a blank page, you'll know what I mean.

According to the writer and actor John Cleese, of Monty Python fame, creativity is as elusive at times as that butterfly passing by you by never landing. It's always just out of your reach, lighting down all around you, but never gracing you with the pleasure of its company.

Surprisingly, research bears out Cleese's observations. Many individuals prefer what scientists call, "the path of least mental resistance." This refers to the act of building on ideas that have already been tried. Another route to this path of least mental resistance is using all the resources they have available, whether they're relevant or not.

When that happens he suggests that you try "trapping creativity." Specifically, he advises, "You have to create boundaries of space and then you have to create boundaries of time." Does that sound like anyone you know? Some of the most creative people claim they work best under pressure.

Many individuals believe for example, that only novels of 100,000 words or more are created. There's a legend that Ernest Hemingway once bragged he could write a creative short story in a mere six words.

Intrigued, his friends took him up on the challenge. Sure enough, in six words he created one of the saddest tales you'll ever read: "For sale: baby shoes, never worn."

Dr. Seuss accepted a similar challenge in his writing, although he agreed to use a few more words. Using a mere 50 different predetermined words, Dr. Seuss wrote a children's book. You've probably read it as a child, read it to your children or even bought it for your niece or nephew. It's called **Green Eggs and Ham.**

While you're probably not writing a short story, you can take a leaf from their book (or story) and think about how constraints on your situation can actually ignite your inner creativity.

How can living in a small apartment and the desire to grow a few vegetables stimulate your outside the box thinking, for example? How could you possibly store all of the kitchen pots and pans you've had when you had a big kitchen now that you've moved into a new apartment with a small galley kitchen? Physical constraints many times are blessings in disguise. If you view them that way from the beginning, perhaps your creativity will kick in even sooner than it normally does.

Remind yourself that there's nothing new under the sun

What does that mean? It means that if you wait until an original, "never used before idea" sneaks up on you, you'll be waiting forever. While certainly there may be a few genuine ideas out there, but they are few and far between.

That may sound depressing until you realize how that can affect you personally. This means that all you need to do is to view the same "dots" as it were and make different connections. That, in effect, brings us back to the origins of the "thinking outside the box" phrase. Remember those nine dots you were asked to connect. How you connected them reflected the state of your creativity at that specific moment in time. You weren't performing any new or creative activity, you were merely trying to "connect the dots" as directed.

Even one of the most creative minds in the electronics age, Steve Jobs, realized that dependency on brand new ideas could spell disaster to your ultimate creative self. He sized up the idea of creative thinking in this way:

"Creativity is just connecting things. When you ask creative people how they did something, they feel a little guilty because they didn't really do it, they just saw something."

The artist, Austin Kleon, said once he is always asked where his ideas from. His honest answer: "I steal them." That's closer to the truth than you may imagine. Ask Twyla Tharp, dancer, and choreographer where she gets her ideas from. She's constantly being inspired by a piece of music or something created from someone else, then she connects the dots, so to speak, in her own way. The result, surprisingly, is a new and sometimes revolutionary creation which becomes an icon in its own right.

Think of West Side Story. If you realize it's "just" a re-working, revision, and update of the Shakespeare's classic, Romeo and Juliet, does it diminish the magnificence of it at all?

The bottom line to this suggestion is to take ideas from others, pretend they're Play-Doh or pliable clay and rework them to suit your needs. The ideas for decor you find on Pinterest may not suit your home exactly, but with a tweak here and a tweak there, the basic idea may work in your home. And viola! By all accounts, you're thinking creatively.

Do something you've never done before

You can immediately see why this works to build your ability to think outside the box. If you've never performed a particular task before, you take a step or two back to figure out the best way for *you* to perform it. Sure, you're going to watch videos, ask others for their advice, but the bottom line is that you're going to work out a plan of attack -- a creative plan of attack -- that works for you. During all of this, you're thinking outside the box without realizing it.

Surround yourself with creative people

This may be a no-brainer, but it is, after all, one of the quickest ways to kick-start your creative thinking. You're around people who think outside of the box almost by second nature. If you not only surround yourself with individuals like this, but watch closely what they do, then emulate them, you'll be thinking outside the box yourself, before you know it.

Remember that, as we noted earlier, that you're the average of the five individuals you frequent the most. If that's the case, then you can't help but find yourself a more creative thinker when you keep company with those whose thought processes are already finely honed in this perspective.

Listen to music

Yes, sometimes it is that easy. Music of any kind actually stimulates the area of your brain that regulates the motor actions, emotions, and -- viola! -- Creativity. According to some studies, the best type of music to have in the background is classical. But, many individuals say that as long as it's the kind of music you love, then it should stimulate your creative stream of thinking.

If you do choose classical music, some researchers suggest listening to anything composed by Mozart. For reasons that aren't entirely clear to researchers, listening to Mozart's compositions can help boost not only your ability to think outside the box, but also strengthen your concentration as well as a few other cognitive functions

This simple, unobtrusive, method may be just what you need to add to your tricks to help think out of the box. Give it a try. What do you have to lose?

The activities listed above should work well for you in getting you accustomed to thinking outside the box and applying a creative vision to your daily life. You may want to implement these one at a time, then sit back and see how they can aid you in your thought processes.

It's possible that some may not work for you. Undoubtedly, though, you'll discover at least one, if not more to boost your thinking.

Conclusion

The methods your mind uses to create your world -- from enhancing your career to chopping onions more efficiently -- is the result of several layers of thought. Many times you employ these layers without being fully consciously aware of them.

While lateral or creative thinking can be the spark that ignites your imagination and sets your passions on fire, you'll still need to implement the other thought processes along your creative journey to piece it all together.

After Einstein used out of the box thinking to visualize himself riding on that beam of light, then he dug in and employed his lateral and critical thinking to ensure his laws of relativity would withstand the critical thinking of his peers.

Without employing critical or lateral thinking, the creativity of Thomas Edison may have been just "wasted" daydreaming.

Even when you go to employ your creativity to problems or changes in your home, you need to layer the types of thoughts you use. All of these different forms of thought processes are needed in order to implement your daily "life hacks" as they're called these days. Sure, that ladder bookshelf sounds like a great idea, but you still need to install it. That's where the other types of thinking are indispensable.

At times, that out of the box thought is essential at the end of a project or a situation. If you read mystery novels or watch crime dramas on television, you will know exactly how this works. The detectives have performed all the critical and lateral thinking needed. They've traced the evidence as far as they could. They've employed logic and then carefully created new ideas and thoughts as they branch off the original evidence.

Yet, they still have hit a dead end. At that point, they take their jigsaw puzzle of clues which is missing one final piece and do something unexpected. They turn the entire puzzle ninety degrees. The result? An entirely different picture appears, usually yielding the big picture allowing the placement of that final missing piece of the puzzle. Now, they clearly see the shape of the puzzle and place it snugly and securely in the hole.

As you become more comfortable with thinking outside the box, you'll become at recognizing when it's needed. In turn, the easier it'll be to call it up when needed.

Thank you for reading this short guide. Now is the time to start thinking outside the box. Try and do your daily tasks differently. Ask completely different questions. Be Creative! Our Imaginations are limitless.

Thank You for Reading Thinking outside the box. As a way to thank you, I have included 2 Chapters of Habits of The Super Rich as a bonus. I hope you will enjoy reading it.

-Bruce Walker

Introduction

"The rich get richer, while the poor get poorer."

"If you're not born rich, you'll never get rich."

"It's impossible to be successful today, there's just too much competition."

Have you heard – or even repeated – any of these adages? If you have, you're not alone. All of us have felt that way at one time or another. But if you take them to heart and say them day after day, they become ingrained in your subconscious and you begin to believe them. These words, which seemed harmless enough when you first started saying them, may have now become a self-fulfilling prophecy.

When that happens, you think that everyone else is successful, regardless of how you define your personal success, but you. The ironic aspect of this is that you can try all sorts of measures from investing in the stock market to online marketing to multi-layer marketing, to – yes! – even playing the lottery. None of this works. At the end of the day, month or year, you haven't seem to make any more money or be any more successful in your career than when you first starting working toward your goal.

Actually, that's not surprising. Some individuals call the use of this mantra so that it's part of your belief system a "self-fulfilling prophecy." It's also known as a "poverty" mentality. They don't have the ability to see themselves as being successful. We all know people like this. Regardless of how hard they work, just they seem to have "bad luck."

Those who have even worked hard in order to work up the economic ladder find, at times, that their mindset holds them back. Imagine the single mom with several children who worked three jobs just to make ends meet. As they grew and she was able to she took courses to become a registered nurse. Today she makes a great income, but still hoards her paycheck and won't pay a utility bill until the companies send a representative to turn off the utility. She has never recovered from her "poverty mentality."

Then there's the other end of the spectrum: the individual who seems to be able to make all the mistakes in the world and still come out successful. No matter what he does he ends up "smelling like roses," as they say.

The Difference Between The Rich and The Poor

In one word: habits!

You can set all the goals you want. To earn $125,000 a year or more. To get that promotion at work. To become a New York Times bestselling author. But unless you have established good habits you'll never reach those goals. Unless you establish the habits of "the rich and famous" you'll forever be chasing success and it will be just slightly out of your grasp.

The real truth is that you can have all that you can have all the riches and success – however, you define them – you wish. There really are no limits to what you can achieve. All you have to do is change your "poverty" mentality to one of success. All you need to do is change the habits that keep you chained to your current lifestyle and your current salary. Swap these habits for better ones, for habits and thoughts and insights that will make you as rich, as successful, as happy as you care to be.

If you're serious about climbing the rungs of success at your workplace, in any online venture or in the entrepreneurial world, then you can do it. And you can accomplish this simply by turning a few bad habits into a few good habits.

The Power of Imitation

That's where this book comes in. This book can succinctly and easily help you recognize and implement that habits the rich and famous use in order to achieve and maintain success. Consider this volume your personal "how to" manual to getting what you desire out of life.

This book is actually only one in a long lineage of classic self-help books. Books like this have been published for years. Probably the most famous is Napoleon Hill's **Think and Grow Rich** or more recently Jack Canfield's **The Success Principles.** If his name sounds familiar, it should. He was one of the editors of the wildly successful books, the first of which was called **Chicken Book for the Soul**. Since then, he and his co-editor Mark Hansen have built that book into a franchise.

Think and Grow Rich author Hill was commissioned by Andrew Carnegie to discover the common habits and traits of the highly successful industrialists of the early twentieth century.

The truth of the matter is that if you visit a bookstore or go to any website that sells books, you'll discover a myriad of self-help books all promising to make you rich.

So why does the world need another book on this topic, this one specifically? Because few, if any, of the reputable books on this topic are written this succinctly. This well-written book gets to the crux of the issue, not only letting you know what the best habits are, how they work and how you can use them to help you "think and grow rich" yourself. In a conversational tone, this volume explains why habits are so very important and how you can effortlessly adopt them.

Not only that, but this book is easy to keep near you, either on your computer desktop, on your ebook reader or both. This means you can refer to it whenever you find your spirit sagging or a dark cloak of pessimism trying to smother you. In these cases, it's easy to pull out this book for inspiration. Before you know, you'll back on track, practicing the good habits all successful individuals do – and knowing that all the universal laws are working toward your success.

It incorporates all the ideas of the classic writers as well as the best of the ideas from today's motivational speakers and books.

What You'll Discover in this Book

This book will show you the habits of the successful and help you put them into practice so that they'll become second nature to you. Not only that, but along with those habits, you'll learn why these habits work, starting with the Universal laws of success. They come in many forms, including the recently celebrated Law of Attraction. Many of you may already be familiar with this from the movie and book, ***The Secret.***

In addition to the law of attraction, there are several other laws that go hand-in-hand with it that can solidify your success for you. These laws a bit less well-known, the laws of detachment, allowing, abundance and gratitude – to name just a few.

You'll also learn the science behind why these habits and perfectly enmeshed. It all starts with the subconscious mind. Equipped with this information, you can go out and initiate any good habit and within the period of your choice, have it become a part of you.

Still don't think any of this is possible? Do you still believe that only a few, the privileged deserve success? If you still think you're "condemned" to live an ordinary life yearning for more, then you need to start reading this book right now.

In the first chapter, you'll vividly see the habits you choose to use can either make or break your success. Why not dig in right now and begin your well-deserved journey to success?

There's no time like the present to change your thinking from "the rich only get richer" to "I am prosperous beyond my wildest imagination."

Chapter 1: Habits of the Rich and the Poor

Jim and Zach had been friends since high school. Both were straight A students. In fact, they graduated sharing the honors as co-valedictorians. There was only one major difference between them, though. Jim didn't need to study. His talent was natural and he soon discovered that a quick look at his lessons was all he needed to get his "A." After that, he turned his attention to recreational pursuits.

Zach, on the other hand, worked hard to keep up with Jim's natural abilities. He found that he needed to study in order to get his good grades. He naturally searched for, developed and perfected habits to help him do just that. Zach knew when to say no to a social invitation in order to study for that important exam, even though it meant missing the good times of a few social engagements.

Throughout their high school career, Jim chided Zach in a good-natured tone about his apparent discipline and the acquisition of his many study habits. Jim took it all in stride saying, "I'll do whatever it takes to get good grades."

Then the pair went off to the same college. It was then Zach's turn to tease his best friend Jim/ Zach was able to take the same habits he had developed in high school and apply them to his college courses.

It's not that Jim was a bad student. Not by any stretch of the imagination. Especially during his first two years. He was able to breeze through the courses, just as he had done in high school.

However, as he got into upper-level coursework he had a bit of trouble here and there. Zach, could see that Jim's academic career may be in danger if he didn't adopt some solid positive habits – and soon.

When graduation day came, Zach had a higher grade point average than Jim. Not by much, but by enough.

As luck would have it, Zach and John received job offers from the same corporation. They worked side by side for several years. But now the tables were turned. Those positive habits Zach had developed in high school and used in college were now the same ones that he needed to prove himself at work.

Jim, though, found it difficult to adjust to the business world. He had not created any substantial good habits during his educational career. In fact, in college, he probably adopted more bad habits than anything else.

Can you guess which proved the better employee? Bingo! Zach. Even though he had to work at everything he did, his habits, by this time, came so naturally to him, that it didn't seem like so much work.

What was worse was that the bad habits Jim had acquired in college carried over to his professional career. Little by little he discovered that he was on a downward spiral.

Bad Habits and the Downward Spiral

If you've never heard of that notorious downward spiral before, think of it as that "slippery slope" so many individuals love to talk about. Let's take the habit of "punctuality," or showing up on time for work. We all can point to someone who is chronically late – to church, to social events, to appointments. While that's irritating, being late to those events aren't career threatening.

Then there are those who are chronically late for work. These are the people who are most at risk of experiencing that downward spiral. You wouldn't think one small habit like being on time could possibly be that crucial in a job. But you'd be surprised where even one small, unassuming bad habit could lead.

If someone were late for work every morning even by ten minutes, his supervisor would eventually note that. Perhaps he may even issue him warnings about it. His supervisor may overlook it if the person were outstanding in his job. But, what if, the individual had the same bad habit of being late in meeting deadlines at work? Turning reports in late, being late to vital meetings – even those that kept important clients waiting.

There's only so much an employer will tolerate. Before you know it, the employer has fired this individual. Think that's the lowest down a spiral can go? Think again. The journey continues. During the time he's off work, he can't find a job, he has trouble meeting his bills and, well, it only goes downhill from there.

All for the lack of one good habit: punctuality.

Let's now look at the flip side of that single habit. Let's assume that this employee, instead, came to work on time every day. How would his career have changed?

Had he done this, his employer would have no need to even give him a warning.

Additionally, if this employee had practiced punctuality, he would have naturally been on time – perhaps even early – for all meetings, turning in all reports and especially for those vital meetings with the company's most important clients.

The Upward Spiral

In the end, he probably would have been a shining example of a model employee and would have been in line for a promotion. With just that one small change in habit, he could have gone from his modest position to a much more lucrative and more responsible position.

There's no need to tell you that as part of that upward spiral, his budding career would have included several salary increases along the way. This means that his personal life also would have been on an upward spiral of a larger house and everything he and his family needed and wanted to create the ideal family life.

Punctuality is just one habit successful people have. If you study the habits of the successful, like the authors Napoleon Hill and later Steven Covey did, you'll find that they hold many of the same good habits.

If you feel as if your life is stagnant and you haven't had the joy of the upward spiral – or worse yet, you recognize you're on that downward spiral -- you may be motivated to seriously scrutinize your habits – right here and right now.

Changing the Direction of the Spiral

Some of us have the mistaken belief that those individuals who have struck it rich and succeeded beyond belief have done so using "dumb luck." That couldn't be farther from the truth, if you scratch the surface, what you discover just below their shiny success, are years of their practicing ingrained good habits.

The good news is that you too can adopt the same habits which made them wildly successful – and become as successful as you desire.

Before you say that it's impossible to change your habits, let's move on to chapter two, which talks about the miraculous power of your subconscious mind and how, with even just a bit of effort, it'll help you not only stop the downward spiral you may find yourself on right now, but actually help you turn the tide and start on an upward spiral.

Chapter 2: Turning thoughts into reality: It All Starts with the Subconscious Mind

The ancestor of every action is a thought.

--Ralph Waldo Emerson

Jim and Zach, our friends from the first chapter, were talking one day. By this point in their careers, Zach was on the fast track – his upward spiral – toward an upper management job.

Jim, on the other hand, was experiencing a downward spiral – and he seemed to be plummeting down that rabbit hole quicker than Alice in Wonderland.

For his part, Jim was in shock, wondering how he could have gotten himself into such a position. "Can I speak honestly with you," Zach offered. After receiving his consent, his pal outlined exactly what he saw.

Jim took a deep breath and said. "It looks pretty hopeless," he said.

Zach immediately corrected him. "It's never hopeless. That is if you're willing to put in some time and effort." Jim immediately agreed.

"Once you take the first step, your subconscious mind will help you the rest of the way."

It's a very simple concept, but one that we tend to overlook. It's one, though, that our friend Zach seemed to know.

When we do acknowledge it we simply underrate it. But it's true. Every building constructed, every book written, every business created first began with some one's thoughts.

Many individuals believe that there's no understanding the subconscious mind. They know ideas pop into their heads, seemingly miraculously, in the middle of the night. They also know that if they don't write them down they seem to dematerialize into a thin cloud of smoke never to be remembered again. The workings of the mind are a mystery, they believe. It's a magical, mystical mystery tour.

Ask anyone who thought with great confidence that they would surely remember this life-changing concept that woke them up without warning at two in the morning. They smiled, simply rolled over and went back to sleep. When the alarm woke them up at 7 a.m., they were so close to recalling the idea . . . but couldn't.

What is the Subconscious Mind?

Your subconscious mind is the repository of the myriad of information that flies by us every day even if we're not aware of them. Our mind catches them in mid-flight and files them away. It's amazing how much information the subconscious mind stores for us, even if we aren't aware we have it stored away somewhere.

But here's a secret about the subconscious that few know. It works best when we're not aware of it working. It's at its most efficient when we aren't alert. That's why we wake up with those wonderful ideas at times. When we sleep we don't have a clue as to what that portion of the mind is doing.

Similarly, it works its magic when we are doing something totally unrelated to what we're working on. How many times have you walked away from a problem or a glitch in a project to have the answering flash in front of you?

No doubt you're well aware of those moments. They may differ from person to person, they may even differ for you depending on the problem and the situation. That's why the eureka moment hits you when you're taking a shower, watching television or even driving a car.

Ever get in a car and drive through an intersection wondering if you really stopped at that red light? Or maybe while you're driving you actually forget to turn on the proper street. That's your subconscious mind working out the details of a project or problem for you.

Ask just about any writer and he'll tell you he gets his best ideas as soon as he opens his eyes in the morning.

Remember those days in grade school and high school when the teacher admonished you for daydreaming? The implication was that you were wasting your time. These days you probably should be doing more of it. Yes, daydreaming is a wonderful way of exercising your subconscious mind. Others find they can put the subconscious mind to work through hypnosis.

The secret about the subconscious mind that all successful people know is that you can use this portion of your brain to your advantage instead of being at the mercy of its seemingly whimsical nature. Through the deliberate use of the subconscious mind, you can use your mind more effectively to influence not only your motivation, but your willpower as well. In fact, once you begin to train yourself in the proper procedure of using this portion of your mind, you'll discover that there's not much you can't do.

How Successful People Put the Subconscious to Work

The following are facts every successful person knows about the subconscious mind. Not only does he know these facts, he works within their bounds so he can make the most of this awesome power.

Subconscious Mind Fact #1: The subconscious mind has no agenda of its own.

This layer of your mind has no will of its own. It doesn't have a "hidden agenda" that is trying to persuade you to its side of an argument or perspective. Its one and only one function:

The subconscious exists solely to produce ideas according to the beliefs and the images you place in it.

Unlike other areas of our brain, such as the ego or the conscious mind, it doesn't judge these images, beliefs or thoughts. Sounds pretty good, doesn't it? You might be thinking right about now that it should be your best friend.

Indeed it should. But then you have to learn that because it doesn't judge, it will manifest anything you place into it. That means it will as readily give you the lack of money you've been thinking about as well as the prosperity you desire. The subconscious mind will hand you illness as quickly as it will hand you health.

To put it in more concrete terms, your subconscious mind is essentially working off the blueprint of your life that you're feeding – whether you realize it or not. It won't stop to examine your thoughts and censor out the negative ones then chastise you for thinking them.

The subconscious mind receives all that you feed it, then begins to bring them to life. Think about it! It could be an awesome tool. If you're thinking prosperity, visualizing the life you dream of, it's not about to judge you. Instead, it quietly goes to work bringing it about. In this way, Emerson was right on the mark. A thought really is the ancestor of every action.

The opposite of this is true as well though. If you go to bed at night – or spend the best part of your day – worrying over your debts, affirming that you live from paycheck to paycheck, then what do you believe your subconscious will deliver you on a silver platter. Exactly what you've been thinking about: more debt.

Instead of finding that fact depressing, you should view it as liberating. Just by changing what you think about – especially right before you go to bed at night and as soon as you wake up in the morning – can actually be the catalyst for the successful life you've been hungering for.

Napoleon Hill knew this in the 1930s when he wrote **Think and Grow Rich.** After interviewing the most productive and most successful business people of his day, he recognized how to use the subconscious mind to produce the success. In his book, he speaks about manifesting "riches" into your life, this same six-step process, based on the nonjudgmental actions of the subconscious mind, can work the same type of magic in your life that it did for others – bring them untold success.

Napoleon Hill's proven Six-Step Process to Success

1. Decide on the specific amount of money you want

This is a very important step. When Hill writes "exact amount' he means it. The more specific you can be in your mind, the better. Don't be wishy-washy about this. Don't waffle. Just decide on how much you want.

Notice I didn't say "need." Don't make the mistake many individuals do at this point in the process. They don't decide on enough. Catherine Ponder a motivational speaker once said, "It's as easy to manifest a button as it is to a castle."

Do yourself a favor from the very beginning, never settle for the button when you really want the castle.

2. Decide what you're going to give in return for receiving this money.

Many people expect at this point money will just rain down from heaven for them, just like in the Old Testament story of the Hebrews in the desert and the manna or bread. Don't expect that you're going to receive your riches by hitting the lottery. Be prepared to start working on an idea – if you haven't already.

Are you going to start offering your services as a writer? Or are you going to start an online business? Now is the time to follow your passion.

3. Establish a deadline.

Go ahead, don't be afraid. You're not going to insult your subconscious mind by presenting it with a deadline. If you don't do this, you'll discover that these "riches" or whatever you desire will always be just out of your reach.

4. Make a detailed plan of action.

Again, don't expect these riches just to fall from heaven. Don't expect your business plan to materialize in front of you with the wave of a magic wand. Instead, you'll want to write out in detail how you plan to carry out your business or your services.

Remember, every good business person started off this way. Think of it as a map. You're here, where "x" marks the spot. There's no use decrying where you are at the moment. Just accept this is your location and your resources for the moment and know – without any reservation of doubt – that you will get to exactly where you'll want to be.

You want to be here, where the map indicates the "treasure" is waiting for you. Besides, a well thought out business plan is the first thing any bank asks for when a person requests a business loan. Where do you plan to be in the next five years? How do you plan to acquire your riches?

That's right. Get a pen and paper. It's better, by the way, to do this initially in long-hand instead of on a computer. This makes it seem more of a serious commitment. Make sure when you do this you include all the necessary facts. This includes the exact amount of money you intend to manifest in your life. Give it a deadline, then write down what services you're going to provide in return for this money. Not only that, but accurately detail the plan you have for bringing all of this to fruition. At this point, you may believe you're done. Not quite.

6. Read this statement twice a day.

Use the power of the spoken word and spend time reading your written account twice a day. Make of a habit of doing this first thing in the morning, before you place any other ideas in your mind and again in the evening, so it's the last idea you think about before going to bed.

But here's the catch. When you do read it, visualize it in your mind. Feel the excitement of success coursing through your body. Believe that the riches you desire, the business you're willing to build to receive it are already manifest in your life. In other words, believe with all the fiber of your body that you already have the money.

TRUTH #2 – The Subconscious can't tell the real from the imagined

For such a potentially powerful organ, the subconscious seems to be "naive." It can't tell the real from the imagined, it only "lives" in the present and understands the present. When people first learn these facts, they try to deny them. After all, your mind is so miraculous, it seems incredulous you can manipulate it so easily.

Think about what was just said. "You can manipulate it – the subconscious mind – so easily." Again, this is difficult to believe. But once you can overcome your disbelief, you may begin to kick yourself. After all, if this is true, then why didn't you learn this earlier in life? It seems like a fairly simple method to help kick-start your success.

As we learn to work with this portion of the brain and learn habits of the rich and famous, you'll discover how important this concept is to your own overcoming bad habits, acquiring good ones and marching forward to success.

TRUTH #3 – The Subconscious only understands the present

The key to true success lies in the "present tense." When you start giving instructions to your brain, you're always going to talk to it in the present tense. When you write out your affirmations, they'll always be written in the present tense. Have you gone through Napoleon Hill's six steps yet? If you have, stop right here and review them. Make sure everything you want is phrased in the present tense. Don't use the future tense.

By now you can probably guess what that would do. That would mean you can see your riches, but they would always be just beyond your reach because you keep asking for them in the future. The future never arrives. By the time it gets here, we call it today. Again, the subconscious is a literal creature.

How Did you get to this Point?

Let's take a step back here for a moment. We should rephrase this. Theoretically, it should be easy to manipulate your subconscious. The problem for many of us, if not all of us, is that others have already manipulated it before we even thought to do this was possible.

Or perhaps you've had a hand in manipulating it yourself and now you have to undo the "damage." What do we mean by that? Perhaps you've been told by your parents growing up that you're not going to succeed in a certain occupation. The competition is fierce and, quite frankly, you're just not smart enough. Think about the field day your subconscious mind had with that statement.

The results? Two possible ones could have manifested. First, you may have avoided that vocation altogether believing that you would never succeed. Or perhaps you were smart enough to ignore your parents and enter the occupation of your dreams only to find yourself failing desperately in it. Why? Because your subconscious mind was already imprinted with the thoughts of failure.

TRUTH #3 - Habits Are the Footprints of the Subconscious

This is an elaborate way of saying that all of your habits are dictated by your subconscious mind. Depending on your point of view, this could be good news or bad news.

Habits are just actions that have been ingrained into our system – some of them since childhood. Think about the habit of brushing your teeth. When you were a youngster your parents probably drilled into you the necessity of that habit. It wasn't something your mind told you to do. But one day, after your parents reminded you for so long, something in your mind clicked. Your parents no longer needed to remind you – and it became a habit.

Ask any person who works at home for a living. These individuals had to establish good habits in order to keep on track every day. These activities are dictated by their job. If it weren't for these "work habits" they never would have been able to sustain such a thriving business.

The truth be told, habits drive all successful people and the subconscious mind drives habits. In order to change your bad habits into good ones, you'll have to manipulate your subconscious. We've already seen that given the attributes of the mind, what may sound difficult, may actually be much easier than you think.

Exercises to Direct the Power of your Subconscious

The beauty of the power of your subconscious is that it is easily trainable. For the longest time, the majority of individuals seeking success were unaware of the power of this awesome aspect of the mind. We thought our bad luck was just that "bad luck." We thought our limited income was somehow dictated by the gods of prosperity or by some fundamental lack of currency in the world.

Neither of these concepts would be further from the truth. Are you ready to start training your subconscious mind to work for you, to bring you your deepest desires, including success in your career and the prosperity that accompanies that, great relationships – both professional and personal – and the power to dictate your moods?

If you've personalized the six steps of Napoleon Hill's found earlier in this chapter, congratulations. You've already taken the first step. But just like exercising any other muscles, you have to perform a variety of exercises to create the habits you'll need in order to get what you want.

The following three exercises will help you reach your goals. You can start using these immediately, while you're reading and studying the rest of this book.

Subconscious Exercise 1: Create Your Vision of a Successful life

Prior to reading this book you probably didn't realize you were the person responsible for the financial or emotional state of your life at this very moment. You may have wanted to blame it on being in the wrong place at the wrong time or a lack of money or even a lack of love.

As we move forward in these chapters you'll learn about the law of abundance. Succinctly this universal law states that there is no lack in the universe, but only an abundance. And it really doesn't matter an abundance of what. You can live the life you've been dreaming of without depriving someone else of their abundant and rich vision of their life. Once you quit thinking that this life is a competition among everyone else you meet or even a rat race, you'll be amazed at how doors, once locked, open easily to your touch.

Even before you learn the workings of this law, you can put it to use. Simply visualize the life you want. That's right! Instead of dwelling on the vision of your life as it is now, begin to imagine the life you want to lead. See it now: the ideal career, the ideal house, the ideal family.

But don't just see it, feel it with every fiber of your body. Get excited about what you're seeing. Feel as if you were living it right now.

Start this visualization process now, and when we talk more about this in a later chapter you'll be that much farther along in the process and, of course, closer to your goals.

When is the best time to visualize? Right before you go to sleep at night and as soon as you wake up in the morning.

Exercise 2: Write Your 10 Goals Daily

Imagine this statistic. Less than three percent of Harvard University students have set goals. At one of the most competitive schools in the nation, that seems to be a small percentage of the students.

Yet, we know that one of the most effective ways to get where you want to go and to enjoy your success is through the creation of goals. If you've thought about setting written goals, you should consider it right now.

Do more than just consider it, though. You should write them down. Think about all the daydreams you've had since you were a child. Consider what you would be doing today if you knew you couldn't fail. If you knew that you could take that leap of faith and succeed, what would you be doing with your life?

Take ten of these goals and write them done. Now, read these out loud several times a day. You may already be a step ahead of me knowing that two of these recitations should be before you go to bed at night and when you wake up in the morning.

Now, take the first step toward one of these goals. You'll see almost immediately your subconscious working perfectly in sync with the universe as events unfold that facilitate you manifesting these long-held desires.

What can't be repeated too many times at this point of your planning is that you must take the first step. You can take it tentatively and hesitantly, that's fine. You can take action with a small measure of doubt that you're actually taking the correct action. The truth is as long as you take action it's the right action.

If it should be the wrong step, your subconscious mind and the universe will work together to set you on the proper path. Guaranteed!

Exercise 3: Use Positive Affirmations to Nourish your Subconscious Mind

This exercise practically goes hand in hand with the previous one. Using those goals you've written, write out positive affirmations that will help you achieve those goals. You're going to create affirmations that, above all, are written in the present tense even though you may not have seen these goals met yet.

For example, I have a friend who has one affirmation is simply: I am a New York Times Best Selling author. She isn't, not yet there. But as you recall her subconscious can't tell the real world from the imagined world. As she recites these words throughout the day, she visualizes what it would feel like to be a bestselling author.

The combination of spoken and written word as well as projecting her emotions into the situation will eventually propel her to that status.

Decide on one or two areas you'd like to work on first. Review your list of goals and create a positive, present tense affirmation to suit your specific needs. This is now yours. Write it out daily and be sure to speak it daily. Yes, especially in the morning when you wake up and in the evening as part of your ritual before you retire.

Believe it or not, you've now created another habit of the successful person. Continue to do this. You may only want to concentrate on one or two affirmations at a time so you can truly focus on them. Congratulations.

In the chapters that follow, we're going to learn more about the laws of the universe, how they work and especially how you can use these to create habits of success and prosperity. But in the meantime begin to put everything you've learned up to now into practice. Your excitement will only mount as you begin to see how your mind is beginning to stir up the long-buried dreams and goals.

Are you ready to continue your success journey? There's no time like the present.

Thank you for reading "Thinking Outside The Box". If you like and find this book helpful. Please take some time to share your thoughts and post a review on Amazon. It'd be greatly appreciated.

I wish you the best and good luck!

Bruce Walker

Made in the USA
Middletown, DE
16 December 2020